The Inside GUIDE

THE MICROSCOPIC WORLD

DNA

Under the Microscope

By Amy Holt

Cavendish Square

Published in 2024 by Cavendish Square Publishing, LLC
2544 Clinton Street, Buffalo, NY 14224

Website: cavendishsq.com

This publication represents the opinions and views of the author based on their personal experience, knowledge, and research. The information in this book serves as a general guide only. The author and publisher have used their best efforts in preparing this book and disclaim liability rising directly or indirectly from the use and application of this book.

Disclaimer: Portions of this work were originally authored by John Shea and published as *DNA Up Close* (Under the Microscope). All new material this edition authored by Amy Holt.

All websites were available and accurate when this book was sent to press.

Library of Congress Cataloging-in-Publication Data

Names: Holt, Amy, author.
Title: DNA under the microscope / Amy Holt.
Description: Buffalo, NY : Cavendish Square Publishing, [2024] | Series: The inside guide. The microscopic world | Includes bibliographical references and index.
Identifiers: LCCN 2022055183 | ISBN 9781502667960 (library binding) | ISBN 9781502667953 (paperback) | ISBN 9781502667977 (ebook)
Subjects: LCSH: DNA–Juvenile literature. | Microscopy–Juvenile literature.
Classification: LCC QP624 .H658 2024 | DDC 572.8/6–dc23/eng/20221212
LC record available at https://lccn.loc.gov/2022055183

Editor: Jennifer Lombardo
Copyeditor: Danielle Haynes
Designer: Deanna Paternostro

Printed in the United States of America

Find us on

CONTENTS

The zebras, giraffes, and plants in this photo all have DNA inside them. The water, sky, and rocks don't.

Chapter One

A WIDE VARIETY

An elephant, a bacterium, and a tree are all very different, but they do have a few things in common. As living things, they all contain one or more cells that hold their DNA. DNA stands for deoxyribonucleic acid, and it holds the instructions for all life on the planet. It controls major things, such as telling trees to grow bark and elephants to grow skin instead of the other way around. It also controls much more specific things. For example, it tells redwood trees to grow tall and birch trees to grow white bark.

Humans have DNA too. It controls just about everything about us through bits of information called genes. There are genes for hair color, skin color, earlobe shape, and even food preferences!

Fast Fact

Cilantro is what we call the fresh leaves of the coriander plant. To many people, cilantro is a tasty addition to some foods. However, some people have a gene that makes them think cilantro tastes like soap.

Discovering Cells

A microbiologist named Robert Hooke was the first person to use the word "cell" in 1665.

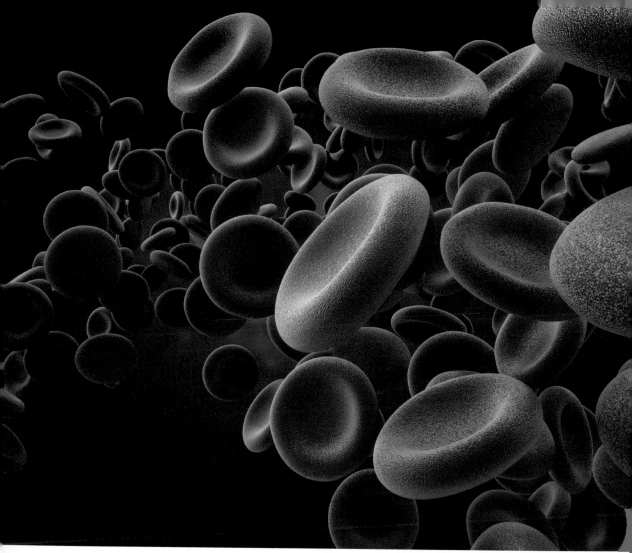

Adult red blood cells are the only cells in the human body that don't have a nucleus or DNA. They lose their nucleus as they grow so they can hold more oxygen.

As he looked at a piece of cork under a microscope, he saw tiny units. He named them cells because they reminded him of the rooms where monks lived, which were also called cells. In 1831, scientist Robert Brown named the central object he saw within a plant cell the "nucleus." Brown's work with plant cells made him think the nucleus was important for cell growth. In 1869, scientist Friedrich Miescher

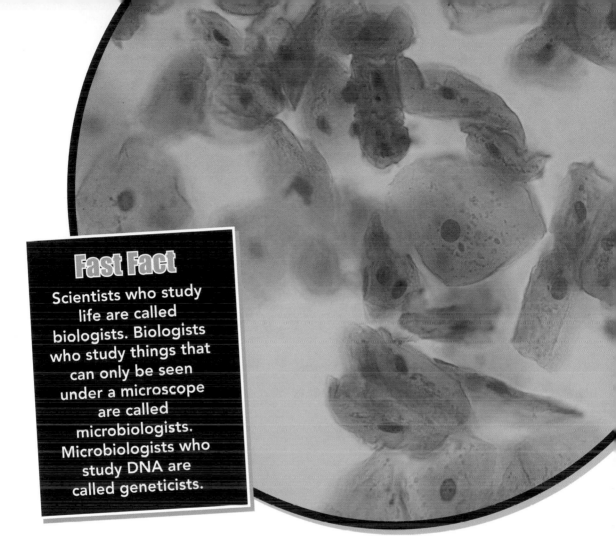

Shown here are human skin cells from the inside of a cheek. The dark circles inside each one are the nuclei (the plural form of "nucleus").

discovered that a substance he named "nuclein" was contained in the nucleus. Nuclein was later renamed deoxyribonucleic acid, or DNA.

What Does It Look Like?

A DNA molecule is a twisted pair of very long, very thin chains of molecules that scientists named nucleotides. These are what we call

NATURE OR NURTURE?

We know genes control everything about our body, but what about our personality? Biologists and sociologists, or scientists who study people, aren't exactly sure how much of what we think and do comes from our genes (nature) or how we grew up (nurture).

Often, nature and nurture go hand in hand. For example, think about the way you speak. Your genes generally determine how high or low your voice sounds, but you probably learned your speech patterns—the way you say certain words—from your parents or guardians. Biologists and sociologists are still finding out more about nature and nurture every day.

the "building blocks" of DNA. Each nucleotide is made up of three separate parts: a **phosphate**, a sugar, and a base. All DNA nucleotides have the same phosphate and sugar, but there are four different bases that connect them to the DNA strand. These are called adenine, thymine, guanine, and cytosine.

The nucleotides form pairs that make up the double helix shape of DNA.

Fast Fact

If the DNA from a single human cell were stretched out, it would be about 6 feet (1.8 meters) in length. There are over 50 trillion cells in your body. All the DNA in your body could stretch from Earth to the sun and back again more than 300 times!

Nucleotides are the "building blocks" of DNA. Just like Legos can be rearranged to make both of these sculptures, the way nucleotides are arranged on a strand of DNA determines what the finished product will be.

Adenine always pairs with thymine, and guanine always pairs with cytosine. The order in which the nucleotides appear is what makes up the instructions.

We talk about genes controlling things about us, but it's more **complex** than it sounds. Each trait, or thing about us, is controlled by hundreds or even thousands of genes, which are made up of many pairs of nucleotides. If this seems confusing, don't worry! Scientists spend years studying DNA, and there are still things they don't understand. The main thing to remember is DNA helps make us who we are.

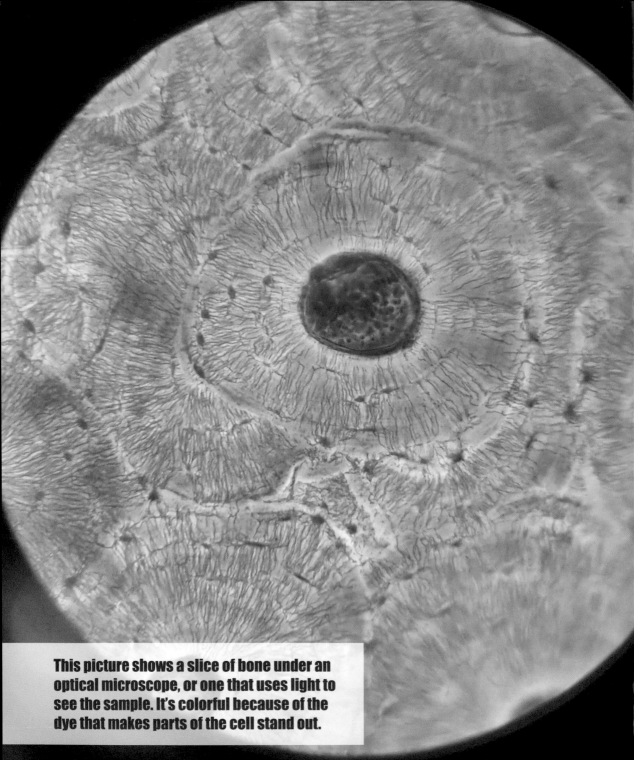

This picture shows a slice of bone under an optical microscope, or one that uses light to see the sample. It's colorful because of the dye that makes parts of the cell stand out.

Science has come a long way since Robert Hooke saw cells under his microscope. Today, we have microscopes powerful enough to let scientists actually see DNA, although not very well. In the future, scientific equipment may become advanced enough to see all the parts of DNA clearly.

In the early days of microbiology and genetics, scientists had to get creative to see the parts of cells, and they often had to make educated guesses about what they were seeing. For example, in the 1800s, scientists found that using dye made parts of the cell stand out. This is how German scientist Walther Flemming first found chromosomes in the nucleus. He named them this because they stained well. ("Chromo" means "color.") Flemming watched these structures as cells divided in two. He observed that the chromosomes doubled, and each new cell received half. Scientists

Fast Fact

In 1931, a man named Ernst Ruska invented the **electron** microscope. This kind of microscope fires tiny particles called electrons at a sample. They're much more powerful than optical microscopes. Some can be used to actually see DNA.

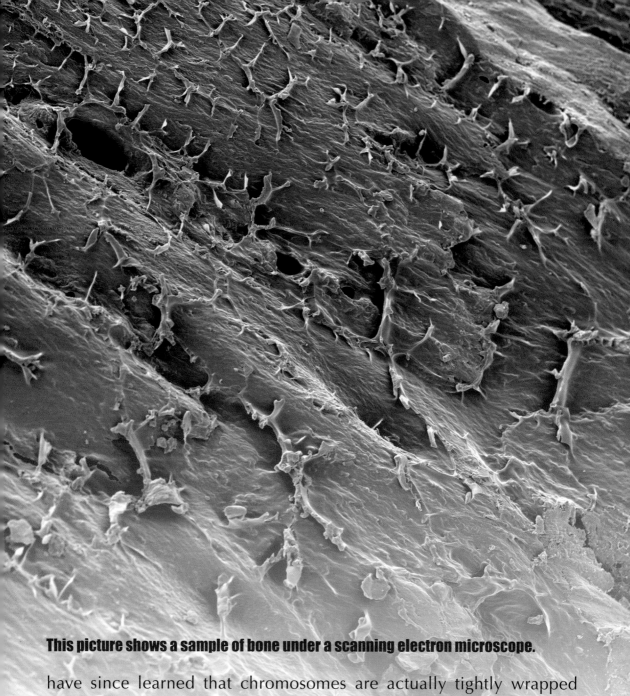

This picture shows a sample of bone under a scanning electron microscope.

have since learned that chromosomes are actually tightly wrapped packages of DNA. They keep those long strands of DNA small enough to fit into dividing cells.

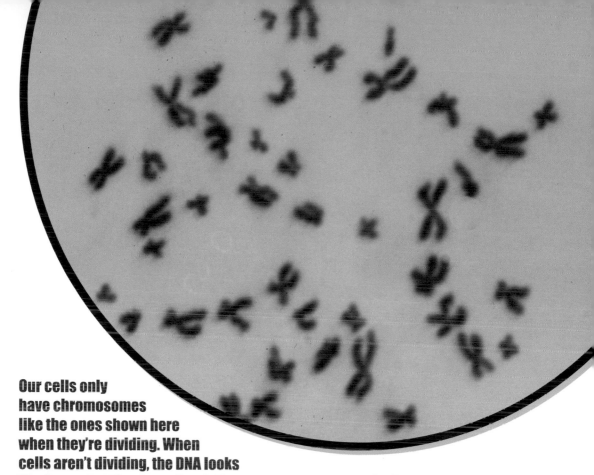

Our cells only have chromosomes like the ones shown here when they're dividing. When cells aren't dividing, the DNA looks like long strands of spaghetti. Chromosomes package the DNA tightly, like twirling that spaghetti around a fork, so it's easier for it to fit in each new cell. When the cells have finished dividing, the DNA becomes long strands again.

Studying and Guessing

By the first half of the 1900s, most scientists guessed that DNA was important for providing instruction to cells, but they had no idea how it worked. They didn't even know what DNA looked like. The molecules were so small they couldn't be seen with the microscopes that were available at the time. Much of the research into DNA depended on studying what it did to the things around it. For example, in 1943, three scientists proved that DNA carries genetic information. They did this by

MITOCHONDRIAL DNA

Most human DNA is found in the cell's nucleus. However, there's a tiny amount found in small structures known as mitochondria. Their DNA tells them to take the energy out of the food we eat and use it as energy to power the cell.

Billions of years ago, bacteria were the only creatures on the planet. At some point, some of them started to evolve, or change over a long period of time. They became the complex cells that form plants and animals—including humans. Scientists have found that much of our mitochondrial DNA is the same as that in bacteria.

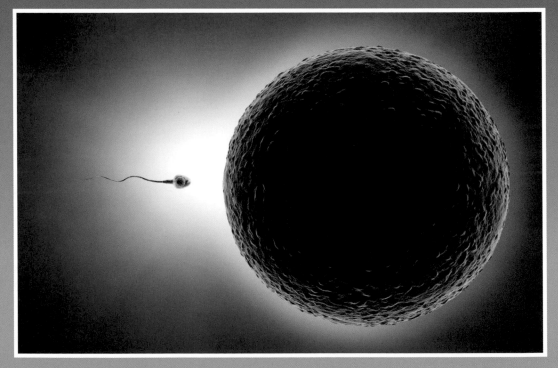

Everyone's mitochondrial DNA comes from their mother. That's because only egg cells (*right*) have mitochondria. Sperm cells (*left*) don't.

adding DNA from a disease-causing bacterium to a harmless bacterium. The DNA turned the harmless bacterium into a disease-causing one.

Franklin, Wilkins, Watson, and Crick

In the 1950s, scientist Rosalind Franklin approached studying DNA in a new way. Franklin shot **X-rays** at DNA and measured how they bounced off. This helped her use math to determine the size and shape of DNA. In 1953, James Watson and Francis Crick, another pair of scientists, looked at Franklin's work without her knowledge or permission. It was Franklin's research that suggested DNA was a double helix and led to Watson and Crick's ideas about DNA's bonds. Watson, Crick, and a third scientist—Maurice Wilkins, who had worked with Franklin in the past—were awarded the Nobel Prize in 1962. Franklin, who died in 1958 at the age of 37, didn't get to share the prize.

In finding out DNA's structure, Watson and Crick also found out how it replicated, or copied, itself. If the bonds between the nucleotides were separated like unzipping a zipper, each strand would act as a pattern for a new, identical strand of DNA. This discovery opened up a brand-new field of science: genetics.

RNA
RIBONUCLEIC ACID

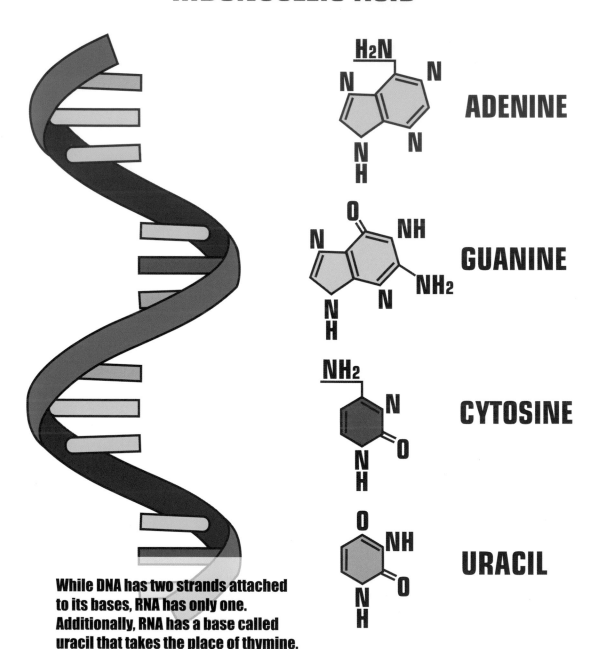

ADENINE

GUANINE

CYTOSINE

URACIL

While DNA has two strands attached to its bases, RNA has only one. Additionally, RNA has a base called uracil that takes the place of thymine.

Chapter Three

DNA AND RNA

DNA works with another substance called ribonucleic acid (RNA) to do its job. The "deoxy" in deoxyribonucleic acid means "less oxygen." Both DNA and RNA are contained in the nucleus in plant and animal cells, which is where the "nucleic acid" part comes from. RNA makes up **organelles** called ribosomes, which make proteins.

Proteins do much of the work in a living thing. They fight disease, carry oxygen, help us move, and form body parts. They also run the chemical reactions that make our bodies work, such as digestion, or the process of breaking down food in the stomach so our cells can use it for energy. There are thousands of proteins in our bodies, each with a special and important job.

Fast Fact

Ribosomes were given their name because they contain RNA. The "ribo" in both deoxyribonucleic and ribonucleic acid stands for the type of sugar that is part of both DNA and RNA. This type of sugar is called ribose.

What Does RNA Do?

A type of RNA called messenger RNA (mRNA) is the "go-between" for DNA and ribosomes. When a cell needs to make a copy of a

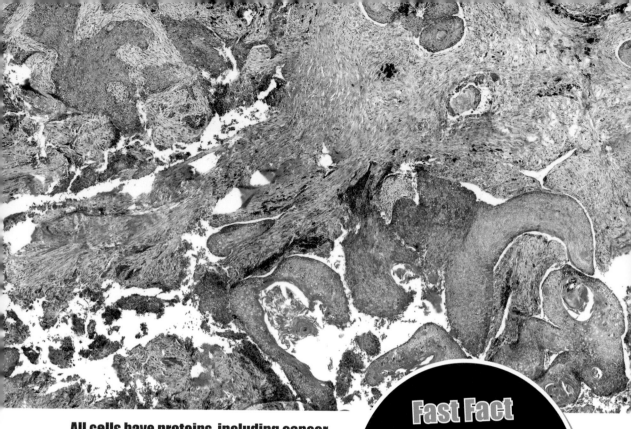

All cells have proteins, including cancer cells. This picture shows the cells of a tumor. The proteins have been dyed red so they show up against the other parts of the cell. By studying the proteins, scientists can learn more about how to fight cancer.

protein, the mRNA takes that information from the cell's DNA. It leaves the nucleus and "delivers the message" to the ribosomes. The ribosomes then use that message like a recipe in a cookbook. The recipe tells them how to make proteins. The "ingredients" of these proteins are called amino acids.

After mRNA brings the recipe to the ribosomes, transfer RNA (tRNA) brings them the ingredients. Then ribosomal RNA (rRNA)—the kind

Some foods—such as beef, fish, eggs, and dairy—are called complete proteins because they have all nine essential amino acids. Foods such as nuts, beans, and grains are called incomplete proteins because they have only some of those amino acids.

inside the ribosomes—uses the ingredients to follow the recipe. It puts the amino acids in the right order to create whatever protein is needed based on what the mRNA told it.

There are 20 amino acids in your body that combine in different ways to make up every part of what we are. The same way you can combine flour, sugar, vanilla, and eggs to make either a cake or cookies, the ways your amino acids combine determine things such as whether your body makes hair or fingernails and where those two materials grow. Not every recipe uses every amino acid.

ALIVE OR NOT?

People like to put things into categories so they're easy to understand. However, sometimes we find something that doesn't fit easily into a category. Viruses are one example. Scientists aren't entirely sure whether they should be considered alive or not. Most have decided to put them in the "nonliving" category.

Living things have DNA, cells, the ability to reproduce, the ability to change over time, and the ability to use energy. Viruses have DNA and do change over time, but they can't reproduce by themselves, they don't have cells, and they don't use energy.

A Secret Code

All living things contain DNA, and all DNA is made from the same four nucleotides. Nearly all living things—from bacteria to trees to humans—also use the same codons when building proteins. Groups of three nucleotides are called codons. Scientists gave them this name because each one contains the code—the "recipe"—for a specific amino acid.

Understanding the sequence, or order, of DNA nucleotides helps scientists and doctors better understand what we're made of, how our bodies work, and what genes cause diseases.

Because all living things contain the same nucleotides and use the same codons, this means that people aren't much different from other animals, genetically speaking. We have about 44 percent of the same genes that fruit flies have and about 90 percent of the same genes mice have. Chimpanzees and humans share 98 percent of their genes. All humans have DNA that's about 99.9 percent similar to each other. No one has exactly the same DNA as another person except identical twins. This is because identical twins are created when one **fertilized** egg cell splits into two different embryos. This is what we call an egg after it's fertilized but before it becomes a baby. Fraternal twins are created when two eggs are fertilized at the same time. Because they started off as two different cells, their DNA is as different as that of siblings who were born at different times.

Fraternal twins can look very similar, but it isn't the looks that determine whether they're identical or not. Identical means "exactly the same," and it refers to the twins' DNA.

Fast Fact

About 98 percent of our DNA doesn't contain genes. In the past, it was called "junk DNA." Researchers now know that these areas determine when a gene should be used.

Some strawberry plants have fish DNA in them that makes them more resistant to cold. This gives us more strawberries because farmers can grow them in colder places. The strawberries don't taste or smell like fish, and they don't affect our DNA when we eat them.

USING DNA

Now that scientists know more about DNA and how it works, they've been able to put it to use in a variety of ways. Today, people use DNA to figure out who has committed a crime, to treat and possibly cure certain diseases, to change food in useful ways, and much more.

Understanding genetics allows us to develop new tools and medications. For example, people with type I diabetes don't make enough insulin, which is a **hormone** produced by an organ called the pancreas. Insulin controls the level of sugar in the blood. Without daily insulin shots, people with this type of diabetes will die. Since 1982, companies have produced insulin safely. Scientists add the human insulin gene to bacteria and yeast. These microscopic organisms continuously produce human insulin as they grow.

Fast Fact

In the past, scientists took insulin from animals' pancreases. Using bacteria and yeast to make insulin has helped save animals' lives as well as humans'.

The Human Genome Project

In 1990, the United States started the Human Genome Project (HGP).

Scientists have used DNA to make other medicines as well, such as the COVID-19 vaccines made by Pfizer and Moderna. These are examples of mRNA vaccines. Scientists used the virus's mRNA to teach our bodies how to make a protein that will tell the immune system to fight the virus if it enters the body. The vaccine doesn't change our mRNA.

Fast Fact

One of the goals of the HGP was to identify disease-causing genes. By studying the sequence of these genes, researchers have a better understanding of certain diseases and have found new ways to treat them.

"Genome" is the word for the complete set of genes present in a living thing. The goal of this project was to identify every single human gene and figure out the order, or sequence, of the nucleotides. The genomes of other organisms, such as bacteria and mice, were also sequenced so they could be compared to the human genome.

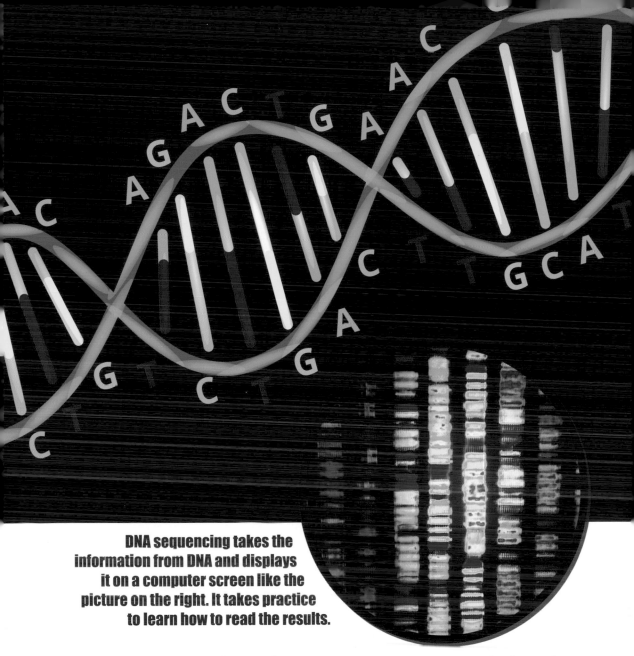

DNA sequencing takes the information from DNA and displays it on a computer screen like the picture on the right. It takes practice to learn how to read the results.

It wasn't long before other countries' scientists, including those from China, France, Germany, Great Britain, and Japan, contributed to the HGP. By April 2003, the HGP had completed its goals—more than 2 years ahead of schedule! It identified about 20,500 different genes and

AT-HOME GENETICS

In recent years, at-home genetic testing kits have seen a huge rise in popularity. Companies such as 23andMe and AncestryDNA send kits to a person's home, and the customer sends their sample back to the company for testing. People use these at-home tests to find out things such as what genetic diseases they might be at risk for and what their **ethnic** makeup is.

Although genetic testing kits can be fun, scientists warn that the results shouldn't be taken too seriously. These kits often produce false results, but even correct results can give someone wrong information. For example, having a gene related to a certain disease doesn't mean that person will definitely develop the disease.

published the sequence of 3 billion nucleotides found in human DNA. The information is free and available online for anyone to use.

Solving Crimes

Forensics is the use of science and technology to help determine facts about a crime. An important part of modern forensics involves DNA. Extremely tiny amounts of DNA left at a crime scene can be recovered by specially trained people to find out whether a suspect was at the scene or not. Over the years, DNA has not only helped find criminals, it has also helped prove the innocence of those falsely accused.

Although DNA is an important crime-solving tool, there are problems with it that make it unreliable. For instance, if more than one DNA sample is present at a crime scene, the DNA could make it look like the wrong person is guilty. Mistakes made by scientists, especially if they're in a hurry or very tired, can produce the wrong results. A damaged sample will also produce bad results. TV shows such as *CSI: Crime Scene Investigation* and *Law & Order* have made many people believe that DNA tells us a lot more than it does. This misunderstanding of how DNA works has been called "the *CSI* effect." Knowing what DNA is, what it does, and how it works is important not only to help us understand our own bodies, but also to make sure it's being used correctly in medicine and forensics.

The 1997 movie *Gattaca* imagined a future in which a person's DNA would determine what jobs they could have.

IN-VALID

010011001-28253

LIVER DISEASE: GTACATGCTAAGTTACCTAACATC
TAGCTTGACCTCCCTGAAGTCACCAGTTCGATGCTTG
GQ 3.4071 - DEFICIENCY LI
SUSP. DE-GENE-ERATE

THINK ABOUT IT!

1. Which parts of you do you think are determined by "nature," and which are determined by "nurture"?

2. What could we learn from seeing DNA more clearly?

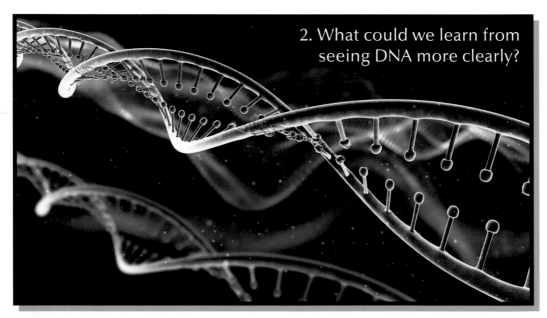

3. How can vegetarians and vegans get enough of all nine essential amino acids in their diet?

4. If it was possible for parents to pick which genes their kids had, would you support this? Why or why not?

GLOSSARY

complex: Having many parts, details, ideas, or functions often related in a complicated way.

electron: A tiny particle in atoms that has a negative charge.

essential: Absolutely needed; impossible to go without.

ethnic: Of or relating to groups of people with common traits.

fertilize: Making something capable of growing and developing.

hormone: A chemical made in the body that tells another part of the body what to do.

organelle: A part of a cell that is necessary for it to carry out its functions.

phosphate: An electrically charged particle that contains the mineral phosphorus.

physiology: A branch of biology dealing with the processes and activities by which life is carried on and which are special features of the functioning of living things, tissues, and cells.

tumor: An abnormal mass of tissue that arises from normal tissue cells and serves no useful purpose in the body.

X-ray: A powerful type of energy that is similar to light but is invisible to the human eye.

Books

Anders, Mason. *DNA, Genes, and Chromosomes*. North Mankato, MN: Capstone Press, 2018.

Ridge, Yolanda. *CRISPR: A Powerful Way to Change DNA*. Toronto, Canada: Annick Press, 2020.

Woollard, Alison, and Sophie Gilbert. *The DNA Book*. New York, NY: DK Publishing, 2020.

Websites

BrainPOP: DNA
www.brainpop.com/science/freemovies/dna
Watch a movie and play games to learn more about DNA.

Ducksters: DNA and Genes
www.ducksters.com/science/biology/dna.php
Read more cool facts about DNA, and test your knowledge with a quiz.

Kiddle: DNA Facts for Kids
kids.kiddle.co/DNA
Check out real photos of DNA as well as 3-D models.

INDEX

A

adenine, 8, 16

amino acid, 18, 19, 20, 29

B

bacteria, 14, 15, 20, 23, 24

Brown, Robert, 6

C

chromosome, 11, 12, 13

Crick, Francis, 15

cytosine, 8, 9, 16

D

disease, 17, 18, 20, 23, 24, 26

E

electron microscope, 12, 15

F

Flemming, Walther, 11

forensics, 26, 27

Franklin, Rosalind, 15

G

genetics, 5, 9, 11, 13, 15, 20, 21, 23, 24, 25, 26, 29

guanine, 8, 16

H

Hooke, Robert, 5, 11

Human Genome Project (HGP), 23, 24, 25

M

messenger RNA (mRNA), 17, 18, 19, 24

Miescher, Friedrich, 6, 7

mitochondria, 14

N

nucleotide, 7, 8, 9, 15, 20, 24, 26

nucleus, 6, 7, 11, 14, 17, 18

P

protein, 17, 18, 19, 20, 24

R

ribonucleic acid (RNA), 16, 17

ribosomal RNA (rRNA), 18, 19

ribosome, 17, 18, 19

T

thymine, 8, 16

transfer RNA (tRNA), 18

U

uracil, 16

V

vaccine, 24

virus, 20, 24

W

Watson, James, 15

Wilkins, Maurice, 15

X

X-ray, 15